G000122616

Uninvited Guests

Gill Lambert

Indigo Dreams Publishing

First Edition: Uninvited Guests
First published in Great Britain in 2017 by:
Indigo Dreams Publishing
24 Forest Houses
Halwill
Beaworthy
EX21 5UU

www.indigodreams.co.uk

ISBN 978-1-910834-45-9

British Library Cataloguing in Publication Data. A CIP record for this book can be obtained from the British Library.

Designed and typeset in Palatino Linotype by Indigo Dreams. Cover design by Joanna Sedgewick.

Printed and bound in Great Britain by 4Edge Ltd
www.4edge.co.uk

Papers used by Indigo Dreams are recyclable products made from wood grown in sustainable forests following the guidance of the Forest Stewardship Council.

For my girls; O, S & N, and my mum,
for their unwavering and total support.
And Mark, for letting me in.

Acknowledgements

My thanks to the publishers who have given life to my poems when I dared to send them into the wider world: *The Interpreter's House, Indigo Dreams Publishing Ltd, Paper Swans Press, Clear Poetry, Algebra of Owls, Poetry Space, The Fat Damsel and Beautiful Dragons Press*. Also to the vibrant local poetry community in Leeds and the surrounding area and the regulars and guests at Sheep Town and Word Club.

Thanks also to the following for their support and guidance in the writing and editing of my work and life in general: Olivia, Sophie and Natasha Lambert, Mick Lambert, Vera Wheeler, Mark and Diana Hardaker, Simon Wheeler, Maria Stephenson, Angela Topping, Rebecca Bilkau and John Mcauliffe. For the use of her incredible photograph for the front cover of this book, I am indebted to Joanna Sedgwick. For specific edits and suggestions for how to make these poems better, special thanks go to Oz Hardwick, Hannah Stone (titles), Amina Alyal and Mark Connors. And to the best friends a girl could wish to have; Laura, Debbie, Nikki and Natalie, my love and eternal gratitude.

Uninvited Guests is Gill's debut solo collection.

An After Dinner's Sleep with Hannah Stone and Maria Stephenson, IDP, 2015.

CONTENTS

Insomnia 5

Backendish 6

Eve 7

Billy's Back 8

Iktsuarpok 10

Trigonometry 11

Questions for Salford Dock 12

Losing My Religion 14

Making Way 15

The Library Boat 16

The Waterfront 17

Rewind 18

February 19

That Kind of Snow 20

Bread 21

Tallow 22

The Woman Who Would Be Your Wife 23

Beds 25

One Night, Right? 26

Bag Man 28

1900 on Grafton St 29

Alive 30

Salt 31

You Wouldn't Know 32

Denim Blue 33

Uninvited Guests 34

When the Swallows Came 35

Insomnia

At three a.m. the words pile in
like noisy teens, loud and lairy
from a night out on the town,
and my mind's a late night
kebab shop – open for business.

Backendish

September beckons, hooks her finger,
promises *mellow* and *ripe* and *full*,
pulls, with mists and chilly mornings,
away from this half-summer,
the pretenders of June and her sisters.
At the same hour each morning
the sun is a little lower as windows steam
with the kettle for a breakfast brew.
The air smells of back-to-school,
new plimsolls and pencils and the smoky,
earthy tang of compost and decay.
Backendish – the last quarter
of the year, the end of the line
of months taking their turn
in reminding me of other years;
concocting the familiar
disguised as something new.

Eve

It began when they were young,
with skin firm as Pippins, flesh
creamy and yielding. She felt it first;
a longing turning to addiction,
the pull of womb on nipples,
prick of desire, sharp as cider.

She gave him her summers; golden days,
delicious afternoons melting into dusk.
He moved under her, dissolving
into her, his seeds scattering on her bed
with its apple wood frame and sheets
as thin as her marriage vows.

Because promises are difficult to keep
when there's nothing else to do but be a wife.
At night she lay in a stifling embrace
and closed her body on serpentine fingers
that found their way in. She woke
to an apathy that lasted till the first bite.

But fermented love grows mould.
His worship of her soured, deceit
of the forbidden turned lust to mush,
with every fall. Her breasts, once ripe
and full, grew wizened like forgotten fruit,
her mouth bruised and purple.

Now she takes her drug in liquid form,
pressed apples tasting of the summers
spent cultivating devotion. Oozing
into her bed, her bloated body desires
nothing now but to drink, craving the high
it gives her, sick from the aftertaste.

Billy's Back

Billy's back.
Back to being a local-hero-boy-made-good
and getting slapped on the back by a Falkland's vet
that his dad, stunned with pride, knew at school.
He's back to waking in his clothes and yawning
pizza boxes on the floor of his room. Back to his mum
overjoyed that he's back, while wishing
at the same time that he'd leave.

Billy's back to boring twats that hang around
the boozer when the drum of beer marches
him away from day-time telly. He's back
to sleeping with his exes 'cos they get off
on the glory that sticks to them. In his mind
he tallies up the dead, along with every drunken fuck,
each frenzied thrust a hole in the head
of the Taliban he's got lined up.

At night he's back to dreaming of his mates
that never made it and to talking to their ghosts.
He's back in Bastion with Jimmy, Ian and Jeff,
their legs blown off, Taffy with his eye out and Nobby
always chatting shite, but now it's all Nobby
can chat.

Billy's back.
Back to Fridays down the pub and Sunday roasts,
back to his mates' pissed-up banter, nights out
after the footy and a shag, if he's lucky,
back to battling through the week and living
for the weekend. And wishing he was back
in Afghan,

waiting for bodies being brought back
in boxes and his best friend, shot to shit

and leaking life into the sand, where he'd left mates
that knew where he was coming from,
didn't ask where he was going, lads that let him be.
Lads that were as desperate to get home,
but now feel just as lonely there
as he.

Iktsuarpok

Sunshine strains to force its way through iron skies
and bring to life a pale day. But still there's no suggestion
of relief from a hundred shades of grey.

The only colour is the red flash of the four-fourteen
from Leeds up to the Dales, rushing to beat the weather,
bearing commuters home to tea and warmth.

The air smells of snow; a crystal cold that threatens
more with every passing hour to stop the day
in its tracks and pin down a year that's gathering pace.

You stop writing to squint at the granite clouds
believing that you see now, or now –
a snowflake, or the picking up of the wind.

You are unsure about the snow and its effect on you,
whether you would rather that it came and kept you here
or if you'd have it never come, so you could leave.

Turn away from the weather.
If there's snow when you turn back
then run outside to greet it, welcome
every whirling feather, hold your face
up to be kissed. You can't delay the snow
or bring it on. Look away.
The snow will come, or not.

*Iktsuarpok is an Inuit word that describes that feeling of anticipation that
leads you to keep looking outside to see if anyone is coming.*

Trigonometry

The boys from school are building houses.
One's on the roof, the other's putting
windows in. Mates now, though back
in class they hardly spoke. Banter
falls and rises through the floors; seeps
into damp plaster on the walls.
Ninety degrees and rising on the tiles, he wipes
the sweat away and smiles as a woman walks past –

he'd know that arse anywhere, though
it's years and years since he was there.
She's not yet past her best and well aware
that she's still turning heads.
Looking up, she sees him, familiar
through the grey and lines of middle age.
It comes back to her – a sweet, brief fling
at seventeen. Lowering her gaze,

she catches another face, framed
in a brand new window.
The earth tilts, her heart rate hits
its apex, a million secrets pass
between them in one look.
Touch and taste and smell in equal
measures. She walks away, her world
back on its axis, their lives in parallel.

Questions for Salford Dock

An ironic death. Five years
of survival counted for nothing
when the winter water put an end
to his heroic return.

What's to blame? The war
for taking him away? The water
that stole the air from his lungs?
His lungs for being so fragile
they surrendered the air
he needed to stay alive? The air
for belching out, deserting him?
His thick wool coat
for dragging him under?

I can find no answers.
The certified copy of the entry
of his death shows the details:
his age, his service number,
rank and regiment. The date
they found his body,
the coroner's name.

Some things I already knew:
his name and date of birth,
the address of the house
where my mother was born.

It's not enough. I trawl
the web, changing search prompts
in a vain hunt for more.
But the net I cast to haul in
news archive or military record
comes back empty. Nothing.

I want more. I want to know
how many died with him,
why it happened, how long
it took for him to perish.
I want an eye-witness, someone
who was there whose account
might lay his ghost to rest.
Only the docks can tell me,
and they're saying nothing.

On January 22nd 1944 my grandfather fell from his boat and drowned as it turned round at night in number 8 dock, Salford.

Losing My Religion
For M.H., after Bahrain

As the clear Middle-Eastern sky spread out the constellations,
he saw the miracle of science – I wavered
on the edge of my belief in God.

Prossecco fuelled the argument, by dawn
and Adhan, he had me convinced; I saw the sense
in having faith in a more logical deity.

We saluted the heavens with our bubbles; two of us,
unbelievers now, with no use for religion, though
I teased him for his use of *Insha'Allah*.

Months later, back home, a message across
the space between us: *After sunset, Venus shines
in the west over the petrochemical complex at Jubail.*

A photograph proves his message: a minute light
above a vast illumination; nature's pin-prick, diminished
against the flaunt of man-made engineering.

Sunset here is ending its spectacle, the trailing edge
of a pale disc fading to a blush behind the horizon.
The bell-practise toll echoes round the valley.

I look towards the west, to Venus,
reliable in the darkening Yorkshire evening,
more dependable than any manufactured God,

then turn to the east and the chant of the Muezzin
to his brothers. Other stars appear, one by one –
angels, to receive my prayers.

Making Way

We share the days between us, *a week*
they said, *perhaps a little more.* We wait,
folding and re-folding our arms and the papers,
stretching our legs in relays, so there's always
someone there, although, by now,
you're mostly sleeping.

When you do wake – briefly – you snap
at her when she tries to make you drink,
an unintentional act which makes her weep.
For the first time in the twenty-six years
I've known you, you have stubble. It's then
I realise, you've already kind of gone.

Yet it's days until you really leave,
going quietly – so unlike you – slipping
away in the early hours, while she holds
your hand. And, I'm sure, at the exact moment
of your shift from one place to another,
new life moves inside me, for the first time.

The Library Boat

Your media circus has no clowns
and no trapeze, but if it did,
I still believe this small crowd
would turn away to greet the boat
that nudges the banks of the Laos.

Celebrations begin, the children grin
welcomes to the crew of three
who unpack boxes of books. One boy
catches your attention, his hands
are like yours might have been once.

Reaching out, his pudgy thumbs
form pincers with his forefingers,
discovering adventures on each side
of the page and his eyebrows raise,
his mouth turns up at every new encounter.

He takes his book and sits in solitude,
savouring his haul, like a small
curled hermit. Your camera goes on
filming him, until the light fades
and Cancer's moon rises.

You bring me this boy's silhouette
one stormy Sunday in December
as I contemplate a turbulent week ahead.
I watch as his book sails him far
from a place I'll never visit.

And as he wrestles with unfamiliar words,
I wonder if my tears are for that boy
who has nothing, yet is satisfied,
or for myself, and this narrow,
cluttered life I have no chance of escaping.

The Waterfront

At times like this I'm pulled back
by nostalgia. It gives me electric blue eyes
and hot-brushed hair, has me teeter
on white stilettos, clip-clopping up

the stairs after last orders at the pubs.
I pay my two quid on the door, hand in
my coat to a fat dragon in a grubby blouse
who's blowing Woodbine down her nose.

Then I'm reeling under neon, white
underwear glowing blue with my gin.
Girls kiss boys in dingy corners, hands
grope in an orgy of tomorrow's boasts and regrets.

Perhaps that's where we all end up,
swaying to Spandau in the top floor room
of a small-town night club. A last dance
in the dark. A last chance to see whether

our costumes really hide the truth, if we can
cover up our youth with grown-up disguises.
And I wonder, when the lights come on,
will we recognise each other?

The Waterfront was a nightclub in Skipton, popular in the eighties.

Rewind

For Jackie Roberts and Megan

Released by murky depth,
the whirlpool will let you go.
You'll rise up onto the bank, stumbling,
pick up your shoes.

Your name will be sucked back
into friends' throats,
they'll wave and your feet will weave
up the steps,

over cobbles and into a bar.
Sambucca shots will leap,
sticky, into glasses,
forward with a flick of an elbow.

You'll un-send the message
telling your friends to go on without you
and delete the pouting selfie
with a boy you won't meet now.

Your drunken shrieks
will be swallowed up by giggling,
your nauseous tilt,
straightened into order.

You'll go home now.
Retrace your steps, backwards
through early evening streets,
tipsy on pre-drinks but steady enough.

Reverse through your front door,
and upstairs, to undress, twice,
uncurl your hair, take off the make-up,
your lipstick smile.

February

Something sticky's on the mouse-pad
and an ex is on 'chat'.
The icon that tells me when the battery is low
isn't working. So I won't know, until the screen fades,
probably just as I pluck up the courage to type *hello*.

The cat's clawing at the wall again
and won't stop until I throw a book at him,
or a pen, and then I'll forget I've thrown it
till I need it again. So I let him scratch –
and he does, with a cat-smile; and tail high
and stretching, he lies down on the keyboard.

The rain is starting again. I'm imprisoned
by a month that somebody should ban.
Too cynical to even worry about roses
never mind expect them. I wonder
whether he'd have got me roses. Perhaps
I should ask before the battery dies.

That Kind of Snow

You had wanted snow,
though not the cruel cold of an Afghan winter,
that crept inside your sleeping bag
and froze the dampness in your socks.
There the snow fell suddenly
on a landscape that you'd come to know,
turning it back into an enemy.

No, not that kind of snow, but
snow that falls here on our hills
and sprinkles tops of walls,
the kind of snow that whispers in the night,
sighing over streets and fields, stays for days,
to disappear in pools of slush.

Your snow lay thick on corrugated iron,
and on flimsy make-shift walls,
where you shivered in the dark,
waiting for a dawn that showed the scars;
conflict; the thief that took whole men
and sent them back in halves, or quarters.

You had wanted soft, expected snow,
the snow that falls in lanes and covers gardens,
where footprints are the proof of destination.

Bread

Dad cuts half-pound slabs
of dough,
kneads two at a time,
drops pairs
in fat-smeared tins.

He stirs the choux,
until it sticks
to the sides of the pan.
Chocolate and cream
melt into thick ganache.

He lines in tempting rows
meringues in snowy peaks
and almond frangipane.

Then the women come,
mill-soiled, cranky
from the early shift,
here for jelly-dripping pies,
warm bread, and buns with icing
that stuff their mouths to a silence
they've waited for all morning.

The afternoon throws shadows
on the bake-house wall,
the oven dies a little,
tomorrow's flour is weighed.
Then he stands over me,
his hands on top of mine,
and helps me knead my own dough.

Tallow

The warden lights the way with lanky strides,
claiming stone steps two by two. The girl
tip-toes through tunnels, catching up with her fate.
Slow down, she could have said – *wait*.
He lopes on, mind on ale-house whores,
fire and food, a blaze of his own.

This candle's hers, to light her night, to watch the hours melt.
Striding at his leisure, he's gone.

Stranded in the stillness, her fingers twist the taper
the Chandler's hands fashioned;
she offers her cheek to the heat to sense some pain.
In the darkness of her final night
the flame is a haloed eye,
a juror with his own verdict; no turning his belief.

Slow down she begs the waxy column – *wait*.
The flame devours the night, tallow pools, wick flickers. Out.

The Woman Who Would Be Your Wife

Remember, when you first laid eyes
on the woman who would be your wife.
The smoke of a youth-club Friday night
made her squint, you winking
when she smiled.

And on the jukebox? You don't know,
Tears for Fears, or something by The Jam.
But girls are good like that, she'd know
that it was *Save a Prayer*
and it became your song.

You don't remember she wore jeans
so tight the denim almost passed as skin,
and that her legs looked good in heels,
lips shining, hair covering her eye,
Phil Oakey style.

She'll remember every single date,
keep bus tickets and tokens from the slots
as she, hip tipped, watched
while you fed machines
with your weekly wage.

She'll keep your letters and your cards,
a necklace in her jewellery box,
a photo that she taped back up
from the nine little squares
she'd torn it into.

When you're forty, say, or fifty,
then you'll remember her: the colour of her eyes,
her breasts under her shirt
with the frilly collar. You'll smile
when you hear her laugh

through the racket of a tap-room Saturday
and spot her in a crowd of friends.
She'll lift her head in recognition,
the woman who would be your wife,
but never was.

Beds

This bed is someone else's; its sheets are crisp Egyptian.
The body next to him, he doesn't know that well,
her smell's still strange. It's not that what she does
is anything he's never had before, just that she does it.
The house is clean and cream; straight lines, sharp corners.

Their bed is older than their marriage,
and before she goes to sleep
she moves a pile of washing from his side,
shoos the cat from off his pillow,
then reads for fifteen minutes while she listens for his car.
And when she doesn't hear it, she lies, wakeful in the dark,
feeling a restlessness she doesn't understand,
then she's guilty for the feeling.

He heaps his unworn gym kit in the wash,
swigs milk straight from a carton.
The shower washes away the scent of the shower
he's just had, that took away the smell of that strange bed.
When he gets in beside her, he rests his wrist on her hip
and his big toe on the back of her heel the way he always does
but when she moves back against him he moves away.
She smells of Johnson's because she shared the baby's bath,
and of familiarity.

One Night, Right?

There's this girl, right?
She's pretty, nothing special,
likes a drink. Good job.
Socialises on Fridays,
sometimes all weekend.
She's tried drugs
but didn't like them.
She'd rather have a drink.

One night, right?
Friday, say, or maybe
on a rare mid-week night out,
she's drinking with her mates
in a pub she's never been to.
She sees a guy, smiles
and he smiles back.
He buys her drinks
all night, and she leaves
with him.
In the morning
she wakes up, this girl,
with a different man.
Not the one from the bar.

So, she can't remember
what happened
but she knows this man
is not the one she left with.
She's nervous now,
wondering who he is
and where the other went.
She dresses, grabs her stuff
and leaves.
She knows, right,
that she'd had a drink

but not that much.
But she keeps quiet,
goes home.

So, three weeks later
and that night,
although still blurry,
becomes more clear.
She feels dirty,
and stays in,
scared of going out.
She drinks alone.

And this girl, right?
She changes everything,
stops wearing make-up,
cuts her hair short,
ditches the mini-skirts,
works and goes straight home.
She runs through that night
in her head, and knows
there's nothing she can do.
She'd had a drink,
so it was her fault.
Right?

Bag Man

He is smaller than he looks.
Underneath his rags he is a brown moth
inside a plump woolly chrysalis.
The wrapping that he wears to keep out the cold
gives no protection from the rain. Wet seeps in,
running salty down his skin and dampness
is the price he pays for distilling his life
into two plastic bags; his past condensed,
reduced to vital details, his future
as uncertain as his next meal.
He contributes his expertise to anyone who'll listen,
pouring his views on their dried-up afternoons
livening a desiccated week-day lunch
with conspiracy theories, the cricket score
and mild swearing. Laughing, he rewards
listeners with his ten black pegs, stripped
of enamel by sugary tea.
This time of year he sits on park benches
and in the cafe that still allows his smell
and his opinion. Dripping onto tiled floors,
fluttering by the gas heater, He's good
at keeping out the cold. But the wet gets in.

1900 on Grafton St

The bowler-hatted man has left his bike
unlocked and propped
outside the shop she's passing.
He's smoking his last drag on his last cigarette
and the camera lets it last forever.
Hand in his pocket, he's got
an opinion he doesn't share.

She looks at me down a hundred years,
more than that.
Her hat is perched on her head
and the effort it takes to hold it there
keeps her back straight.
Her dress is black, or peacock, or sienna.
That's her secret.
Her chin juts, she's purposeful,
Victorian-Edwardian; she's both, or neither.

When she gets home, a girl
will take her coat, make the tea.
She'll discuss the evening meal
with an older woman.
She might sit for a while
in the silence of a life
she knows is good. It is.
Everything is black and white.

Alive

Probably, it's a little thing, like the rain.
A certainty, like a gas bill or a snag
in a stocking that runs to a ladder.
Or a coincidence, like Mandela
dying on the same day as the premier
of a film about his life.

Often it's a bigger thing, like the death
of someone you know, or a bomb
in a city you'd only ever heard of,
never been to, with whole families dead.
Or a flood, miles away in a Cornish village,
where a man has lost his wife.

Usually it's the smallest thing, like dust,
a rainbow in January, or a song
that reminds you of the very last time
you felt like this.

Salt

Home means the same whether there or here,
the desert or city; belonging, safety.
Clothes laid out on a bed for school,
or to flee from the hell it's become.

Hate feels the same when it's born of the fear
of an enemy, a friend who has turned away,
or the uninvited, the unexpected,
the frightening masses of misunderstood.

Sanctuary's the same when you feel it near,
a bed, a box, a stranger's hand,
the opening door of a house that's full
but with room enough for more.

Salt tastes the same whether wave or tear,
whoever cries for a displaced child,
whichever tide washes his body
with the rhythm of the moon.

You Wouldn't Know...

When he woke this morning
he turned and pressed against her,
she smiled in her sleep –
asked for five more minutes.

He spilled his coffee, tie-dye
on the pristine white, he took
the staircase two steps at a time
to see her naked, stopped to kiss her.

Tender fingers tucked the label
in the collar of a clean shirt,
smoothed the fabric down over
the contours of his shoulders.

When he crossed over the road
and turned into the station,
he was looking at her picture,
her smile was all that he took with him.

In the moment of the bomb blast,
he was thinking of his children,
the things they'd do this weekend,
though it was only Tuesday.

Denim Blue

'And though you want him to last forever,
you know he never will…' Cat Stevens – *Oh Very Young*

The sand's the same – biscuit darkening
to caramel, brown sugar, dissolving
into cappuccino foam. The café's there,
from where you'd buy your endless
cups of tea, but the polystyrene cups
have gone. Now they're selling
Fair Trade in recycled cardboard –
pasties from an artisan.

A thwack from someone's tennis ball
against a cricket bat, like when
you slogged ours for a six. Then,
my heels kicked up the beach,
you stood and laughed, flares
flapping at your ankles; jeans
with patches spelt your love for them.

Dads are building sandcastles,
towels mark their boundaries,
windbreaks battering and crackling.
Surfer dudes with dreadlocks and tattoos
scan a turquoise sea that deepens
to the indigo horizon, then denim blue,
fading up to the sky.

The waves erase my footprints.
I'm leaving nothing behind,
it only makes the goodbye harder.

Uninvited Guests

I sat until the light went, reading
other people's poetry and trying
to make some sense out of my own.

Eventually I raised my head
to pink clouds and a black stain
of nameless birds moving

over the spring sky, perhaps
coming home in answer
to a change in the air.

I've had an hour of near
silence, but now muffled squawks
of neighbours' voices pushing

through walls remind me
of my own family's needs.
For a while, nothing else matters

but *who wants carrots?*
and reuniting odd socks with their siblings.
Later I'll look at the few words

I've written and rescue my fragile
eggs of thought, smothered
by fat cuckoos in a nest of meaning.

When the Swallows Came
For Mark

Birds disturbed her; they tapped at fastened glass,
flapping wings and gripping handles
with their talon feet. They pecked
at sun-warmed putty, loosening the panes.

Jackdaws cawed their morning songs
in high-up branches, thrushes lined
with Monday's washing. Fat rosy robins
stared at her from jet-bead eyes,
so she pulled the blinds, blocked them out
like Christmas in July.

She slammed the sashes down
and locked them, hiding tiny keys in places
she forgot. In winter, a rook as black as soot
came hurtling down the chimney; she wrapped it
in plastic, put it out into the white.

So, when the swallows came, she almost didn't hear them,
taking their streaming for summer drizzle.
She watched them through the glass, their rides
of air and skies telling tales of longer days
and warmer nights. She forgot her fear of feathers,
flung her windows wide.

Now, starlings explode upwards, fused
with giddiness, curlews circle, house martins
clag their homes against her walls. At night,
a kingfisher picks at her eyes and fills them
with a blue she doesn't recognise.

The swallows plummet skylights, dive
through rooms, up and out again. She gulps
them in, and now she knows the sound she hears
outside her window is not always the rain.

Indigo Dreams Publishing Ltd
24, Forest Houses
Cookworthy Moor
Halwill
Beaworthy
Devon
EX21 5UU
www.indigodreams.co.uk